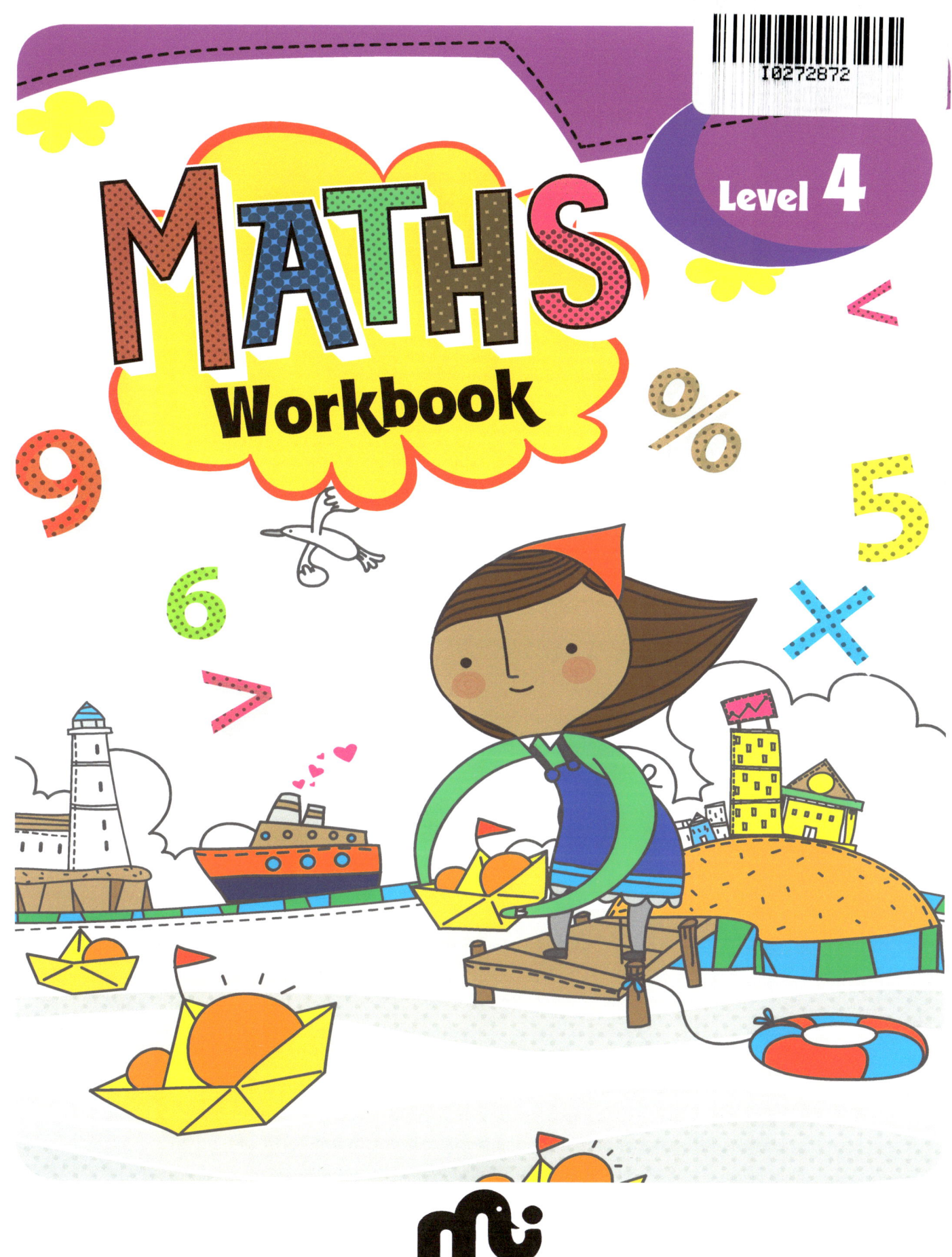

Published in Moonstone
by Rupa Publications India Pvt. Ltd 2022
7/16, Ansari Road, Daryaganj
New Delhi 110002

Sales centres:
Allahabad Bengaluru Chennai
Hyderabad Jaipur Kathmandu
Kolkata Mumbai

Copyright © Rupa Publications India Pvt. Ltd 2022

The views and opinions expressed in this book are
the authors' own and the facts are as reported by them
which have been verified to the extent possible,
and the publishers are not in any way liable for the same.

All rights reserved.
No part of this publication may be reproduced, transmitted,
or stored in a retrieval system, in any form or by any means,
electronic, mechanical, photocopying, recording or otherwise,
without the prior permission of the publisher.

ISBN: 978-93-5520-718-0

First impression 2022

10 9 8 7 6 5 4 3 2 1

The moral right of the authors has been asserted.

Printed in India
This book is sold subject to the condition that it shall not,
by way of trade or otherwise, be lent, resold, hired out, or otherwise
circulated, without the publisher's prior consent, in any form of binding
or cover other than that in which it is published.

Contents

Numbers 4

Adding Numbers 9

Subtraction 13

Multiplication 18

Division 23

Factors and Multiples 28

Fractions 33

Test Yourself 39

Geometry 42

Answers 45

Numbers

A. Use the Indian place value chart and write the number names for the following.

1. 356179 = _____

2. 4026498 = _____

3. 7948060 = _____

4. 2100784 = _____

5. 6345019 = _____

B. Use the International place value chart and write the number names for the following.

1. 4905318 = _____

2. 6472009 = _____

3. 1040306 = _____

4. 5171120 = _____

5. 887403 = _____

C. **Complete the number patterns.**

1. 24308, 24409, 24510, _____, _____, _____
2. 3470961, 3472961, 3474961, _____, _____, _____
3. 708294, 707295, 706296, _____, _____, _____
4. 67548, 167548, 267548, _____, _____, _____
5. 869076, 859076, 849076, _____, _____, _____

D. **Use the Indian place value chart to mark the periods by placing the commas. Complete the table by writing the period, place and place value of 7 in the following.**

	Number	Period	Place	Place Value
1.	74,695	Thousands	Ten thousand	7 × 10,000 = 70,000
2.	388742			
3.	8470091			
4.	7211500			
5.	5087602			
6.	76994			

E. **Write the numerals in the expanded form.**

1. 14325   = _____

2. 260048 = _____

3. 876690 = _____

4. 7829653 = _____

5. 122359 = _____

F. Write the following in the short form.

1. 3 × 100000 + 8 × 10000 + 2 × 1000 + 5 × 100 + 6 × 10 + 9 × 1 =
_____

2. 9 × 100000 + 7 × 1000 + 6 × 100 + 2 × 10 + 3 × 1 =
_____

3. 2 × 1000000 + 2 × 10000 + 8 × 1000 + 5 × 1 =
_____

4. 7 × 100000 + 6 × 10000 + 5 × 1000 + 4 × 100 + 3 × 10 + 2 × 1 =
_____

5. 1 × 100000 + 8 × 10000 + 5 × 1000 + 2 × 10 + 7 × 1 =
_____

G. Mark the periods and compare the numbers using > , < or =.

1. 64297 ☐ 64927
2. 2441697 ☐ 2414679
3. 75420 ☐ 8194
4. 3871129 ☐ 9371182
5. 59463 ☐ 50946
6. 642790 ☐ 4420769

H. Form the smallest and greatest numerals using the given digits.

Digits	Greatest number	Smallest number
1. 5, 0, 1, 7, 6, 3		
2. 8, 7, 8, 9, 2, 4		
3. 0, 4, 2, 6, 7, 1, 9		
4. 3, 4, 1, 8, 4, 2, 7		
5. 8, 9, 6, 0, 5		

I. Fill in the blanks with the correct answer.

1. The predecessor of the greatest 7-digit number is _____.

2. The successor of the greatest 6-digit number is _____.

3. The successor of the smallest 7-digit number is _____.

4. The predeccessor of the smallest 5-digit number is _____.

5. The place value of 8 in 286429 is _____.

6. The difference in the face values of 5 in 452506 is _____.

7. One million in International system of place value is equal to _____ in the Indian system of place value.

8. Hindu-Arabic numerals for XLV is _____.

9. The difference of the greatest and the smallest numeral formed using the digits 9, 7, 0, 4, 8, 3 is _____.

10. The correct numeral for eight lakh eight thousand eight hundred and eight is _____.

J. Round off the following numbers to the nearest 10.

1. 38 _____   2. 647 _____

3. 372 _____   4. 80746 _____

5. 73210 _____   6. 4274 _____

K. Round off the following numbers to the nearest 100.

1. 3622 _____   2. 9745 _____

3. 54093 _____   4. 4866 _____

5. 16332 _____   6. 64558 _____

L. Round off the following numbers to the nearest 1000.

1. 62900 _____   2. 19726 _____

3. 210476 _____   4. 74298 _____

5. 38435 _____   6. 87529 _____

M. Write the following in the Hindu-Arabic numeral system.

1. XCV _____   2. CCLIII _____

3. CMVII _____ 4. CDXX _____

5. LXXXII _____ 6. LIV _____

N. Answer the following in Roman numerals.

1. How many days are there in a leap year? _____

2. How many hours are there in a day? _____

3. An hour has _____ minutes.

4. There are _____ bones in an adult's body.

5. There are _____ items in a dozen.

6. There are _____ years in a decade.

7. One century has _____ years.

8. One kilogram has _____ grams.

Adding Numbers

A. **Add the numbers using the expanded form. See the example given below.**

1. 21783 + 46215 = $\boxed{67998}$

   21783 = 20000 + 1000 + 700 + 80 + 3
   + 46215 = 40000 + 6000 + 200 + 10 + 5
   _____   _____
               60000 + 7000 + 900 + 90 + 8 = $\boxed{67998}$

2. 45245 + 35826 = _____

3. 356857 + 139215 = _____

4. 686181 + 241867 = _____

B. Arrange the given numbers in columns and add them.

1. 214810 + 410475 + 145392

2. 36439 + 43282 + 21859

C. Fill in the blanks keeping the rules of addition in mind.

1. (4675 + 2274) + 1423 = (1423 + 4675) + _____

2. 19267 + (37298 + 53342) = 37298 + (_____ + 19267)

3. 57162 + 93851 + 0 = 93851 + _____ + 57162

4. 72347 + 62438 + 18970 = 18970 + 72347 + _____

5. 89604 + 1000 = _____

6. 274893 + 100 = _____

7. 197248 + 10000 = _____

8. 766425 + 10000 = _____

9. 367290 + 0 = _____

10. 492369 + 1 = _____

D. Find the estimated sum and actual sum for the following.

1. 42849 and 46135

   Estimated sum = _____

   Actual sum = _____

2. 72739 and 16423

   Estimated sum = _____

   Actual sum = _____

3. 41244 and 58649

   Estimated sum = _____

   Actual sum = _____

E. Solve the word problems given below by writing the statement and the answer.

1. A motor vehicle company sold 24678 vehicles in year 2014 and 19245 vehicles in year 2015. What was the total number of vehicles sold in both the years?

   _____

   _____

   _____

2. Meera has 7468 caps, 2375 stamps and 3429 marbles. What is the total number of items collected by her?

   _____

   _____

   _____

3. A train covered 45283 km distance on day 1 and 27640 km distance on day 2. What was the total distance covered by the train?

_____

_____

_____

_____

4. There are 25623 language books, 39724 science books and 35280 maths books in a school library. How many books are there in all?

_____

_____

_____

5. Two groups collected funds of $13849 and $28677 respectively. What is the total amount of money that they have?

_____

_____

_____

Subtraction

A. Arrange the numbers in columns and subtract them.

1. 67984 − 39478

2. 242172 − 81690

3. 89742 − 9934

4. 78000 − 36425

B. Use the rules of subtraction to fill in the blanks.

1. 46789 − 100 = _____

2. 7342 − 0 = _____

3. 640080 − 1 = _____

4. 29654 − 1000 = _____

5. 783364 − 100000 = _____

6. 56420 − 1 = _____

7. 812475 − 10000 = _____

8. 23658 – 23658 = _____

9. 33640 – 0 = _____

10. 14503 – 14502 = _____

C. Find the estimated difference and actual difference for the following by subtracting.

1. 32734 from 64298

    Estimated Difference = _____

    Actual Difference = _____

2. 53890 from 70000

    Estimated Difference = _____

    Actual Difference = _____

3. 28640 from 87320

    Estimated Difference = _____

    Actual Difference = _____

D. Solve the following using subtraction.

1. The number which is 2764 less than the largest 4-digit number. _____

2. The number which is 48925 less than the smallest 6-digit number. _____

3. The number which should be added to 71048 to make it the largest 5-digit number. _____

4. The difference between the largest 5-digit number and the smallest 7-digit number. _____

5. The number which should be subtracted from 728645 to get 708645. _____

6. The difference between the smallest 6-digit number and the largest 6-digit number. _____

E. Solve the word problems given below by writing the statement and the answer.

1. 467890 people were travelling by a train. If 2389 of them get down at a station, how many people are still in the train?

   _____

   _____

   _____

2. A lady earns $64270 per month. If she saves $17800 at the end of the month, how much money did she spend?

   _____

   _____

   _____

3. A dealer bought a vehicle for $452600 and sold it for $487500. How much money did he save?

   _____

   _____

   _____

4. After getting a scholarship of $30500, Reena still has to pay a sum of $12870 for the school fee. What is the total fee of her school?

   _____

   _____

   _____

5. A company cut down 13450 trees to build their factory. As a replacement, they planted 54200 trees around the town. How many more trees were planted by the company?

_____

_____

_____

F. Write two subtraction facts for each of the following addition facts.

1. 61245 + 23687 = 84932

   _____ and _____

2. 34755 + 53210 = 87965

   _____ and _____

3. 19815 + 21236 = 41051

   _____ and _____

4. 23218 + 41265 = 64483

   _____ and _____

G. Subtract and check the answer.

1. 300000 − 164284 = _____

2. 278645 − 38429 = _____

3. 867004 − 340862 = _____

H. Solve the following using addition and subtraction.

1. What number should be subtracted from 25000 to get 14286? _____

2. Which number is 16235 more than the number 47819? _____

3. What number should be added to 386518 to get 835681 as sum? _____

4. What number should be subtracted from 318964 to make it smallest 6-digit number? _____

5. How much bigger is 34789 than the number 6800? _____

6. What should be added to the largest 5-digit number to make it largest 6-digit number? _____

7. Find the minuend if the subtrahend is 63087 and the difference is 30726. _____

8. Find the subtrahend if the minuend is 10000 and the difference is 6481. _____

I. Fill in the missing digits in the given problems.

1.
TTh	Th	H	T	O
1	7		6	4
+ 4	3	3	2	
			6	7

2.
TTh	Th	H	T	O
4	9		7	4
−		8	3	8
2		2		0

3.
TTh	Th	H	T	O
7	3		6	
−		0	1		4
0		6	2	5

4.
L	TTh	Th	H	T	O
1	3	0	1		7
+		5		4	4	3
7		2	6		9

5.
TTh	Th	H	T	O
7	9	8	5	0
−			3	0	0
	5	6			

6.
TTh	Th	H	T	O
2	0		3	6
+			9	4	3
3		8		6

Multiplication

A. Write the missing factor or product.

1. _____ × 8 = 72
2. 97 × _____ = 970
3. 38 × 8 = _____
4. 11 × 1 = _____
5. 64 × 20 = _____
6. 56 × _____ = 56
7. 58 × 1 = _____
8. 85 × _____ = 0
9. 12 × _____ = 108
10. 18 × 5 = _____
11. 100 × 10 = _____
12. _____ × 15 = 150

B. Arrange the given numbers in columns and find the product.

1. Multiplicand = 8014
   Multiplier = 9

2. Multiplicand = 3059
   Multiplier = 16

3. Multiplicand = 8465
   Multiplier = 13

4. Multiplicand = 16428
   Multiplier = 20

5. Multiplicand = 7474

    Multiplier = 16

6. Multiplier = 2605

    Multiplicand = 19

C. **Multiply the given 2-digit numbers by writing them in a lattice. See the example given below.**

1. 46 × 35

    (40 + 6) × (30 + 5)

	40	6
30	(30×40) 1200	(30×6) 180
5	(5×40) 200	(5×6) 30

    Now, add the numbers.

    46 × 35 = 1200 + 200 + 180 + 30 = 1610

2. 58 × 21

3. 73 × 49

4. 66 × 33

5. 25 × 84

D. Use multiplication to solve the following.

1. The product of 58 and its successor is _____.

2. The product of the greatest 3-digit number and the smallest 4-digit number is _____.

3. By adding 384 to itself 15 times, you will get _____.

4. The product of 97 and its predecessor is _____.

5. There are _____ minutes in a day.

E. Multiply the numbers. Write the correct letter with each answer to solve the riddle.

	4	7	5	2	E
	×			3	

		8	4	5	A
		×		9	

	1	3	6	4	0	N
	×				8	

	2	4	8	9	C
	×			7	

	3	6	0	8	L
	×			5	

	3	8	4	1	D
	×			6	

I am tall, when I am young. As I get old, I become shorter.

I am a _____.

| 17423 | 7605 | 109120 | 23046 | 18040 | 14256 |

21

F. Solve the word problems given below.

Working Space

1. The ticket for a ride costs $18 for one person. How much money would be collected if 1598 tickets were sold during the fair?

2. There are 25 rows of trees in a garden. If every row has 489 trees, how many trees are there in all?

3. A donation event was organised for which every block donated 5680 things to orphanages. If 18 blocks participated in the event, how many things were collected for the donation?

4. The monthly school fee is $6425 per child. How much fee will be paid by each child for a whole year?

5. How many days are there in 18 years if neither of them is a leap year?

6. 1236 groups of dancers applied to participate in a dance show. If each group has 22 dancers, how many people have applied for participation in all?

7. A box contain 5550 matchsticks. How many matchsticks will be there in 23 such boxes?

Division

A. Use division and its properties to answer the following.

1. 8697 ÷ 8697 = _____
2. 48000 ÷ 4 = _____
3. 2800 ÷ 28 = _____
4. 18645 ÷ 0 = _____
5. 9532 ÷ 1 = _____
6. 365 ÷ 10 gives quotient = _____ and remainder = _____
7. 7620 ÷ 100 gives quotient = _____ and remainder = _____
8. For 256000 ÷ 256 quotient = _____ and remainder = _____
9. 572 ÷ 11 = _____
10. 0 ÷ 426 = _____
11. 8760 ÷ 876 = _____
12. 2800 ÷ 100 = _____

B. Complete the table given below using division.

S. No.	1	2	3	4
Dividend	480		248	364
Divisor	6	12	5	8
Quotient		7		
Remainder		0		

C. Divide the numbers using long division to find the quotient and the remainder.

1. 5384 ÷ 15

   15) 5384

   Q = ☐

   R = ☐

2. 4208 ÷ 18

   18) 4208

   Q = ☐

   R = ☐

3. 5081 ÷ 13

   13) 5081

   Q = ☐

   R = ☐

4. 12485 ÷ 22

   22) 12485

   Q = ☐

   R = ☐

D. Use short division method to solve the following. See the example given below.

1. 289 ÷ 8

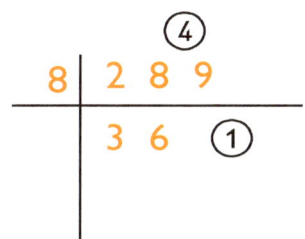

Q = 36

R = 1

2. 548 ÷ 9

Q = ☐

R = ☐

3. 362 ÷ 5

Q = ☐

R = ☐

4. 279 ÷ 7

Q = ☐

R = ☐

E. Use unitary method to solve the given problems.

Working Space

1. 5 doughnuts cost $75. What will be the cost of 8 such doughnuts?

   Answer: _____

2. 8 packets of popcorn cost $72. How much will 12 such packets cost?

   Answer: _____

3. The rent of a house for one year is $64800. What will be the rent of the same house for 7 months?

   Answer: _____

4. Manav buys 13 apples for $91. How many apples can be bought for $112?

   Answer: _____

5. The weight of 11 watermelons is 264 kg. Assuming that every watermelon is of the same weight, how much will 6 watermelons weigh?

   Answer: _____

6. A man made 57 baskets in 3 hours. How many baskets can be made in 20 hours?

   Answer: _____

7. A tailor needs 540 m cloth to make 90 dresses. How much cloth will she need to make 35 dresses?

   Answer: _____

F. **Estimate the quotient and find the actual quotient.**

1. 97 ÷ 19

   Estimated quotient = _____

   Actual quotient = _____

2. 84 ÷ 12

   Estimated quotient = _____

   Actual quotient = _____

3. 108 ÷ 11

   Estimated quotient = _____

   Actual quotient = _____

4. 548 ÷ 18

   Estimated quotient = _____

   Actual quotient = _____

G. **Write the multiplication fact for the given division statement and division facts for given multiplication statements.**

(a)	Division statement	Multiplication fact	
(1)	966 ÷ 21 = 46	(1)	
(2)	3105 ÷ 9 = 345	(2)	
(3)	1250 ÷ 25 = 50	(3)	
(b)	Multiplication statement	Division fact	
(1)	147 × 12 = 1764	(1)	
(2)	89 × 25 = 2225	(2)	
(3)	505 × 19 = 9595	(3)	

Factors and Multiples

A. Fill in the blanks with the correct word.

1. A _____ is a number which divides the given number completely.

2. A _____ is the product of two or more numbers which are not fractions.

3. _____ is a factor of every number.

4. The lowest multiple and the highest factor of a number is _____.

5. All _____ numbers are divisible by 2.

6. Factors of 10 are 1, _____ , _____ and _____.

7. _____ is called a unique number.

8. _____ is the only even prime number.

9. Numbers with only two factors 1 and the number itself are called _____ numbers.

10. Numbers which have more than two factors are called _____ numbers.

B. Write all the factors of the given numbers.

1. 25 _____

2. 42 _____

3. 77 _____

4. 36 _____

5. 81 _____

C. Write the first five multiples of the given numbers.

1. 8, _____, _____, _____, _____, _____.

2. 10, _____, _____, _____, _____, _____.

3. 3, _____, _____, _____, _____, _____.

4. 15, _____, _____, _____, _____, _____.

5. 12, _____, _____, _____, _____, _____.

D. Write the factors of the number pairs and find the common factors.

1. 27, 36

   Factors of 27 are _____

   Factors of 36 are _____

   Common factors of 27 and 36 are _____

2. 15, 40

   Factors of 15 are _____

   Factors of 40 are _____

   Common factors of 15 and 40 are _____

3. 8, 44

   Factors of 8 are _____

   Factors of 44 are _____

   Common factors of 8 and 44 are _____

4. 14, 84

   Factors of 14 are _____

   Factors of 84 are _____

   Common factors of 14 and 84 are _____

E. Write all the multiples of 6 which lie between 25 and 45.

_____

_____

F. Write all the multiples of 13 which are less than 150.

_____

_____

G. Write three common multiples of the given number pairs.

1. 5 and 10 _____

2. 2 and 3 _____

3. 6 and 10 _____

4. 4 and 8 _____

5. 1 and 7 _____

H. Use factors and multiples to find the answers of the questions given below.

1. A number which is a factor of 36 but not a multiple of 2? _____

2. An even number which is a factor of 30. _____

3. An odd number which is a factor of 18. _____

4. The first even multiple of 13. _____

5. A number which is an odd factor of 55. _____

6. A number which is a factor of 42 and a multiple of both 2 and 3? _____

7. A number which is a factor of 39 but not a multiple of 3? _____

8. The difference between the third and sixth multiple of 14. _____

I. **Write the factors of the given numbers and tell whether they are prime or composite. The first one has been done for you.**

Number	Factors	Prime or Composite
1. 22	1, 2, 11, 22	Composite
2. 71		
3. 98		
4. 91		
5. 43		
6. 39		
7. 55		
8. 89		

J. **Read the sentences and write "factor" or "multiple" to form the correct sentences.**

1. 7 is the smallest _____ of the number 7.

2. 12 is greatest _____ of the number 12.

3. 5 and 9 are two _____ of the number 45.

4. 18 and 42 are the _____ of number 6.

5. Every number is a _____ of 1.

K. **Find the HCF and LCM of the following numbers.**

1. 9 and 117   HCF _____, LCM _____

2. 45 and 81   HCF _____, LCM _____

3. 98 and 7   HCF _____, LCM _____

4. 2 and 40   HCF _____, LCM _____

5. 15 and 80   HCF _____, LCM _____

L. Check the divisibility of the numbers below by 2, 3, 5 and 10. Put (✓) or (X) to show your answer.

Numbers	2	3	5	10
75				
40				
18				
56				
300				
925				
84				
81				

M. Find the prime factorization of the following numbers using the factor tree method.

1.
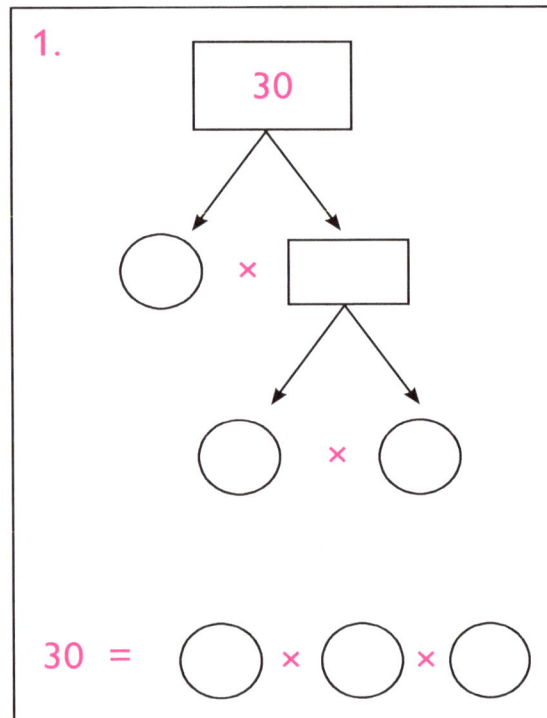

2.
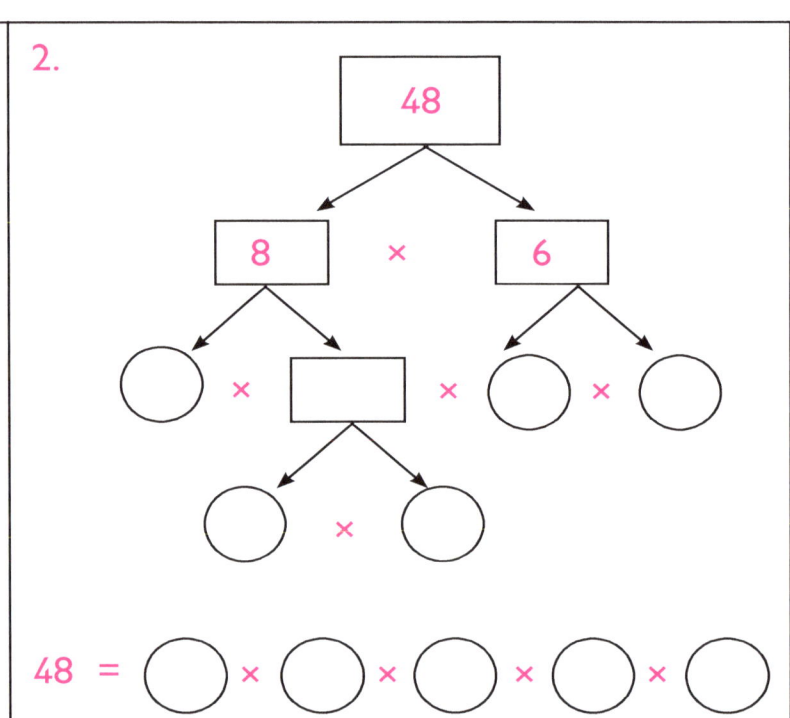

Fractions

A. Write the fraction of the shaded portion of the figures given below.

(a)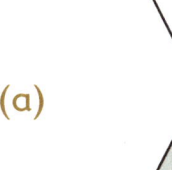

(b)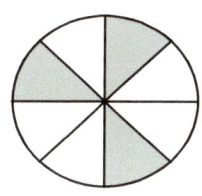

(c)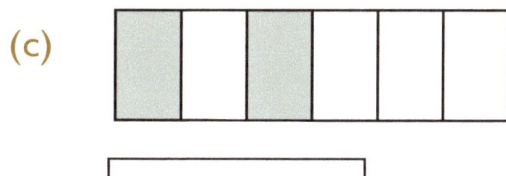

(d)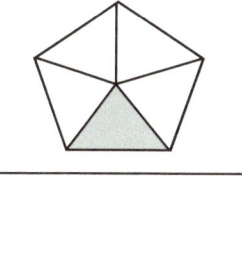

B. Identify and circle the proper fractions among the following.

(a) $\dfrac{1}{9}$ (b) $\dfrac{2}{5}$ (c) $\dfrac{8}{3}$ (d) $\dfrac{4}{7}$ (e) $\dfrac{9}{8}$

C. Which of the following are improper fractions? Circle them.

(a) $\dfrac{12}{7}$ (b) $\dfrac{3}{5}$ (c) $\dfrac{5}{2}$ (d) $\dfrac{6}{9}$ (e) $\dfrac{7}{6}$

D. Write a like fraction for each of the following.

(a) $\dfrac{1}{3}$ ☐ (b) $\dfrac{4}{5}$ ☐ (c) $\dfrac{2}{9}$ ☐ (d) $\dfrac{7}{10}$ ☐

E. Which of the following are unit fractions?

(a) $\dfrac{3}{7}$ (b) $\dfrac{1}{4}$ (c) $\dfrac{6}{9}$ (d) $\dfrac{1}{3}$ (e) $\dfrac{1}{15}$

F. Write the missing number such that the new fractions are equivalent to the given fraction.

(a) $\dfrac{3}{7} = \dfrac{\Box}{21} = \dfrac{6}{\Box} = \dfrac{12}{\Box}$

(b) $\dfrac{1}{2} = \dfrac{5}{\Box} = \dfrac{\Box}{22} = \dfrac{7}{\Box}$

(c) $\dfrac{4}{5} = \dfrac{\Box}{15} = \dfrac{36}{\Box} = \dfrac{60}{\Box}$

(d) $\dfrac{6}{11} = \dfrac{\Box}{44} = \dfrac{42}{\Box} = \dfrac{\Box}{110}$

(e) $\dfrac{2}{7} = \dfrac{\Box}{84} = \dfrac{26}{\Box} = \dfrac{18}{\Box}$

G. Express the following mixed numbers as improper fractions.

(a) $3\dfrac{1}{7} = \Box$

(b) $5\dfrac{3}{5} = \Box$

(c) $2\dfrac{4}{7} = \Box$

(d) $4\dfrac{8}{10} = \Box$

(e) $5\dfrac{1}{6} = \Box$

(f) $6\dfrac{2}{9} = \Box$

(g) $5\dfrac{1}{7} = \Box$

(h) $3\dfrac{4}{3} = \Box$

(i) $1\dfrac{6}{5} = \Box$

(j) $6\dfrac{3}{4} = \Box$

H. Use cross multiplication to find out which fraction is smaller than the other.

(a) $\dfrac{4}{7}$ ☐ $\dfrac{3}{9}$

(b) $\dfrac{3}{5}$ ☐ $\dfrac{6}{10}$

(c) $\dfrac{9}{11}$ ☐ $\dfrac{9}{8}$

(d) $\dfrac{6}{10}$ ☐ $\dfrac{3}{10}$

I. Convert the following improper fractions into mixed numbers.

(a) $\dfrac{15}{4}$ ☐ (b) $\dfrac{29}{8}$ ☐

(c) $\dfrac{47}{7}$ ☐ (d) $\dfrac{87}{9}$ ☐

(e) $\dfrac{20}{3}$ ☐ (f) $\dfrac{56}{9}$ ☐

J. Compare the fractions given below using the signs >, < or =.

(a) $\dfrac{5}{5}$ ☐ $\dfrac{1}{5}$ (b) $\dfrac{2}{7}$ ☐ $\dfrac{5}{7}$

(c) $\dfrac{5}{9}$ ☐ $\dfrac{4}{9}$ (d) $\dfrac{3}{8}$ ☐ $\dfrac{7}{8}$

(e) 1 ☐ $\dfrac{1}{4}$ (f) $\dfrac{3}{10}$ ☐ $\dfrac{9}{10}$

(g) $\dfrac{6}{5}$ ☐ $\dfrac{2}{5}$ (h) $\dfrac{1}{3}$ ☐ $\dfrac{1}{3}$

(i) $\dfrac{9}{11}$ ☐ $\dfrac{10}{11}$ (j) $\dfrac{1}{5}$ ☐ $\dfrac{3}{5}$

K. Reduce the following fractions to their lowest terms.

(a) $\dfrac{4}{36}$ ☐ (b) $\dfrac{6}{42}$ ☐

(c) $\dfrac{3}{39}$ ☐ (d) $\dfrac{8}{88}$ ☐

(e) $\dfrac{7}{35}$ ☐ (f) $\dfrac{12}{60}$ ☐

(g) $\dfrac{21}{49}$ □ (h) $\dfrac{18}{81}$ □

(i) $\dfrac{20}{35}$ □ (j) $\dfrac{12}{96}$ □

L. Solve the following and find the lowest term of the answer in each.

(a) $\dfrac{4}{9} + \dfrac{2}{9}$

(b) $\dfrac{3}{14} + \dfrac{5}{14}$

(c) $\dfrac{7}{6} + \dfrac{4}{6}$

(d) $\dfrac{8}{7} - \dfrac{1}{7}$

(e) $\dfrac{9}{15} - \dfrac{4}{15}$

(f) $\dfrac{12}{10} - \dfrac{4}{10}$

M. Read the statements and solve the problems.

(a) A pizza was divided in 8 equal slices. If Raman ate 5 slices, what fraction of pizza is left?

(b) Somya completed $\frac{2}{5}$ of her work in the morning and $\frac{1}{5}$ of her work in the afternoon. She decided to complete the rest of her work in the evening. How much work did she have to do in the evening?

Test Yourself

A. Find the HCF and LCM for the following sets of numbers.

1. 15 and 75   HCF _____ , LCM _____

2. 8 and 136   HCF _____ , LCM _____

3. 40 and 10   HCF _____ , LCM _____

4. 12 and 20   HCF _____ , LCM _____

5. 7 and 42   HCF _____ , LCM _____

B. Find the prime factorization of the given numbers by using the factor tree method.

1. 75

2. 88

C. Find the first 3 common multiples of the following numbers.

1. 3 and 6 :   _____ , _____ , _____

2. 7 and 2 :   _____ , _____ , _____

D. Write all the common factors of the given numbers.

1. 36 and 14 _____

2. 50 and 30 _____

E. Check the symbol and solve each of the following. Give answer in mixed fraction if possible.

1. $\dfrac{6}{15} - \dfrac{1}{5}$

2. $\dfrac{8}{9} + \dfrac{1}{3}$

3. $1\dfrac{2}{4} + 4\dfrac{3}{4}$

4. $1\dfrac{5}{6} - 1\dfrac{1}{2}$

F. Solve the following word problems.

1. Sam ate $\dfrac{1}{6}$ part of a cake. His family had $2\dfrac{1}{3}$ cake. If there were three cakes, how much is still left?

2. A vendor sold $6\frac{1}{4}$ kg vegetables in the first half of the day and another $3\frac{1}{3}$ kg in the second half of the day. How much vegetables did he sell throughout the day?

3. Half of a herd of cows went to graze in a field. One-fourth of the herd went near the river and rest of the cows are still inside the farm. What fraction of cows are there in the farm?

4. Meenu gave away $\frac{2}{5}$ of her chocolate to her brother and $\frac{2}{5}$ to her sister. If she still has $1\frac{1}{5}$ chocolate with her, how much chocolate did she have before sharing it?

Geometry

A. See the figures given below and name the lines, line segments and rays.

1.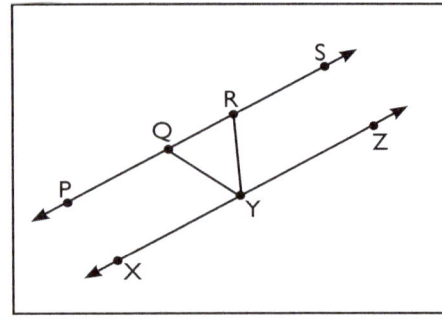

   Lines _____

   Line segments _____

   Rays _____

2.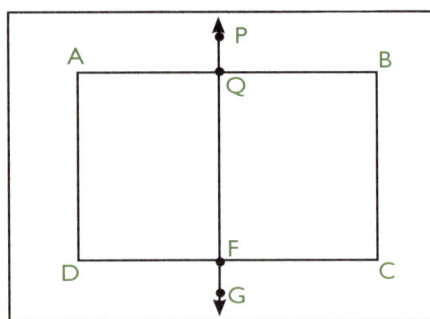

   Lines _____

   Line segments _____

   Rays _____

B. Fill in the blanks to form correct sentences.

1. A ray has _____ end point.

2. A line segment has _____ end points.

3. A _____ can be extended on both the sides.

4. _____ lines are always at an equal distance from each other.

5. The point at which two rays or line segments meet forms an _____.

6. A _____ is a closed figure made up of straight line segments.

7. Polygons with 4 sides are called _____.

8. The diameter of a circle is twice its _____.

42

9. The distance from any point on the circle to its center is called its _____.

10. The length of a circle is called its _____.

C. Label the parts of a circle and name them.

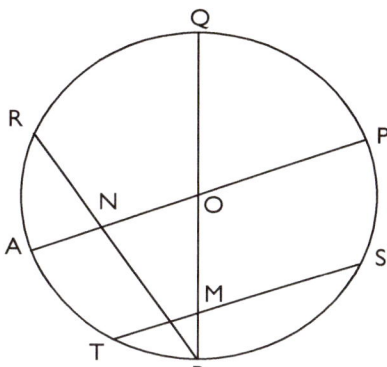

The Centre _____

A Radius _____

A Diameter _____

A Chord _____

D. Name the different parts of the given figures.

1. The angle _____

   The arms of the angle _____

   The vertex _____

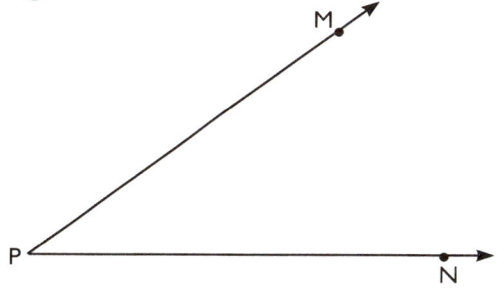

2. The triangle _____

   The rays _____

   The line segment _____

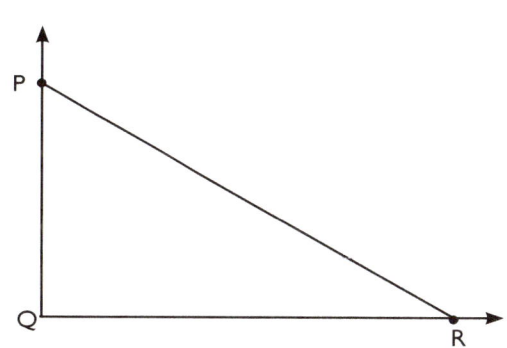

3. The angle _____

   The vertex _____

   The rays _____

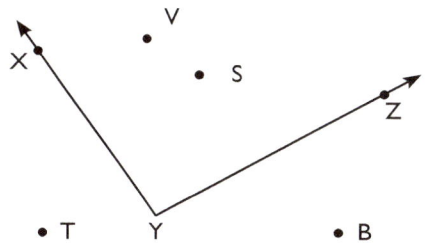

   The points in the interior of the angle _____

   The points in the exterior of the angle _____

E. Draw and label the following polygons.

A triangle	A square
A rectangle	A hexagon

Answers

Numbers

A. 1. Three lakh fifty six thousand one hundred seventy nine.
2. Forty lakh twenty six thousand four hundred ninety eight.
3. Seventy nine lakh forty eight thousand sixty.
4. Twenty one lakh seven hundred eighty four.
5. Sixty three lakh forty five thousand nineteen.

B. 1. Four million nine hundred five thousand three hundred eighteen.
2. Six million four hundred seventy two thousand nine.
3. One million forty thousand three hundred six.
4. Five million one hundred seventy one thousand one hundred twenty.
5. Eight hundred eighty seven thousand four hundred three.

C. 1. 24611, 24712, 24813
2. 3476961, 3478961, 3480961
3. 705297, 704298, 703299
4. 367548, 467548, 567548
5. 839076, 829076, 819076

D. 1. Thousands, Ten Thousand, 7 × 10,000 = 70,000
2. Hundreds, Hundred, 7 × 100 = 700
3. Thousands, Ten Thousand, 7 × 10,000 = 70,000
4. Lacs, Ten Lacs, 7 × 10,00,000 = 70,00,000
5. Thousands, Thousand, 7 × 1,000 = 7,000
6. Thousands, Ten Thousand, 7 × 10,000 = 70,000

E. 1. 10000 + 4000 + 300 + 20 + 5
2. 200000 + 60000 + 40 + 8
3. 800000 + 70000 + 6000 + 600 + 90
4. 7000000 + 800000 + 20000 + 9000 + 600 + 50 + 3
5. 100000 + 20000 + 2000 + + 300 + 50 + 9

F. 1. 382569 2. 907623
3. 2028005 4. 765432
5. 185027

G. 1. < 2. > 3. >
4. < 5. > 6. <

H. 1. 765310, 103567
2. 988742, 247889
3. 9764210, 1024679
4. 8744321, 1234478
5. 98650, 50689

I. 1. 9999998 2. 1000000
3. 1000001 4. 9999
5. 8 ten thousands 6. 0
7. Ten lakh 8. 45
9. 682641 10. 808808

J. 1. 40 2. 650 3. 370
4. 80750 5. 73210 6. 4270

K. 1. 3600 2. 9700 3. 54100
4. 4900 5. 16300 6. 64600

L. 1. 63000 2. 20000 3. 210000
4. 74000 5. 38000 6. 88000

M. 1. 95 2. 253 3. 907
4. 420 5. 82 6. 54

N. 1. CCCLXVI 2. XXIV
3. LX 4. CCVI
5. XII 6. X
7. C 8. M

Adding Numbers

A. 1. 67,998 2. 81071
3. 4,96,072 4. 9,28,048

B. 1. 7,70,677 2. 1,01,580

C. 1. 2,274 2. 53,342

3. 0   4. 62,438   3. 73769 − 70144 = 3625

5. 90,604   6. 274,993   4. 130176 + 652443 = 782619

7. 2,07,248   8. 7,76,425   5. 79850 − 23300 = 56550

9. 3,67,290   10. 4,92,370   6. 20436 + 19430 = 39866

D. 1. 90000, 88984   2. 90000, 89162

3. 100000, 99893

Multiplication

A. 1. 9   2. 10   3. 304

E. 1. 43923   2. 13272   3. 72923 km

4. 11   5. 1280   6. 1

4. 100627   5. $42526

7. 58   8. 0   9. 9

10. 90   11. 1000   12. 10

Subtraction

B. 1. 72126   2. 48944   3. 110045

A. 1. 28506   2. 160482

4. 328560   5. 119584   6. 49495

3. 79808   4. 41575

C. 2. 1218   3. 3577   4. 2178

B. 1. 46689   2. 7342

5. 2100

3. 640079   4. 28654

D. 1. 3422   2. 999000   3. 5760

5. 683364   6. 56419

4. 9312   5. 1440

7. 802475   8. 0

E. CANDLE

9. 33640   10. 1

F. 1. $28764   2. 12225 trees

C. 1. 30000, 31564   2. 20000, 16110

3. 102240 things   4. $77100

3. 60000, 58680

5. 6570 days   6. 27192 dancers

D. 1. 7235   2. 51075   3. 28951

7. 127650 matchsticks

4. 900001   5. 20,000   6. 899999

Division

E. 1. 465501 people   2. $46470

A. 1. 1   2. 12000   3. 100

3. $34900   4. $43370

4. not defined   5. 9532   6. 36, 5

5. 40750 trees

7. 76, 20   8. 1000, 0   9. 52

F. 1. 84932−61245 = 23687

10. 0   11. 10   12. 28

    84932−23687 = 61245

B. 1. Q = 80, R = 0   2. D = 84

2. 87965−53210 = 34755

3. Q = 49, R = 3   4. Q = 45, R = 4

    87965−34755 = 53210

C. 1. Q = 358, R = 14   2. Q = 233, R = 14

3. 41051−19815 = 21236

3. Q = 390, R = 11   4. Q = 567, R = 11

    41051−21236 = 19815

D. 2. Q = 60, R = 8   3. Q = 72, R = 2

4. 64483−23218 = 41265

4. Q = 39, R = 6

    64483−41265 = 23218

E. 1. $120   2. $108

G. 1. 135716   2. 240216   3. 526142

3. $37800   4. 16 apples

H. 1. 10714   2. 64054   3. 449163

5. 144 kg   6. 380 baskets

4. 218964   5. 27989   6. 900000

7. 210 m

7. 93813   8. 3519

F. 1 5, 5   2. 8, 7

I. 1. 17364 + 43323 = 60687

2. 49674 − 28384 = 21290

3. 10, 9   4. 25, 30

G. a. 1. 46 × 21 = 966
2. 345 × 9 = 3105
3. 50 × 25 = 1250

b. 1. 1764 ÷ 147 = 12
2. 2225 ÷ 25 = 89
3. 9595 ÷ 19 = 505

3. factors   4. multiples
5. multiple

K. 1. HCF = 9, LCM = 117
2. HCF = 9, LCm = 405
3. HCF = 7, LCM 98
4. HCF = 2, LCM = 40
5. HCF = 5, LCM = 240

L. 75: 3, 5, 10
40: 2, 5, 10
18: 2, 3
56: 2
300: 2, 3, 5, 10
925: 5
84: 2, 3
81: 3

M. 1. 30 = 2 × 3 × 5
2. 48 = 2 × 2 × 2 × 2 × 3

Factors and Multiples

A. 1. factor   2. multiple
3. 1   4. itself
5. even   6. 2, 5, 10
7. 1   8. 2
9. prime   10. composite

B. 1. 1, 5, 25   2. 1, 2, 3, 6, 7, 42
3. 1, 7, 11, 77   4. 1, 2, 3, 4, 6, 8, 9, 12, 18, 36
5. 1, 3, 9, 27, 81

C. 1. 16, 24, 32, 40, 48   2. 20, 30, 40, 50, 60
3. 6, 9, 12, 15, 18   4. 30, 45, 60, 75, 90
5. 24, 36, 48, 60, 72

D. 1. 1, 3, 9   2. 1, 5
3. 1, 2, 4   4. 1, 2, 7, 14

E. 30, 36, 42

F. 13, 26, 39, 52, 65, 78, 91, 104, 117, 130, 143

G. 1. 10, 20, 30   2. 6, 12, 18
3. 30, 60, 90   4. 8, 16, 24
5. 7, 14, 21

H. 1. 3, 9   2. 6, 2   3. 9, 3
4. 26   5. 11, 5   6. 6
7. 13   8. 42

I. 1. 1, 2, 11, 22; composite
2. 1, 71; Prime
3. 1, 2, 7, 14, 49, 98; composite
4. 1, 7, 13, 91; composite
5. 1, 43; prime   6. 1, 3, 13, 39; composite
7. 1, 5, 11, 55; composite
8. 1, 89; prime

J. 1. multiple   2. factor

Fractions

A. (a) $\dfrac{1}{4}$ (b) $\dfrac{3}{8}$ (d) $\dfrac{2}{6}$

(e) $\dfrac{1}{5}$

B. (a) (b) (d)

C. (a) (c) (e)

D. (a) $\dfrac{2}{6}$

(b) $\dfrac{8}{10}$

(c) $\dfrac{6}{27}$

(d) $\dfrac{21}{30}$

E. (b) (d) (e)

F. (a) $\dfrac{3}{7} = \dfrac{9}{21} = \dfrac{6}{14} = \dfrac{12}{28}$

(b) $\dfrac{1}{2} = \dfrac{5}{10} = \dfrac{11}{22} = \dfrac{7}{14}$

(c) $\dfrac{4}{5} = \dfrac{12}{15} = \dfrac{36}{45} = \dfrac{60}{75}$

(d) $\dfrac{6}{11} = \dfrac{24}{44} = \dfrac{42}{77} = \dfrac{60}{110}$

(e) $\dfrac{2}{7} = \dfrac{24}{84} = \dfrac{26}{91} = \dfrac{18}{63}$

G. (a) $\dfrac{22}{7}$ (b) $\dfrac{28}{5}$ (c) $\dfrac{18}{7}$

(d) $\dfrac{48}{10}$ (e) $\dfrac{31}{6}$ (f) $\dfrac{56}{9}$

(g) $\dfrac{36}{7}$ (h) $\dfrac{13}{3}$ (i) $\dfrac{11}{5}$

(j) $\dfrac{27}{4}$

H. (a) > (b) = (c) < (d) >

I. (a) $3\dfrac{3}{4}$ (b) $3\dfrac{5}{8}$ (c) $6\dfrac{5}{7}$

(d) $9\dfrac{6}{9}$ (e) $6\dfrac{2}{3}$ (f) $6\dfrac{2}{9}$

J. (a) > (b) < (c) > (d) <
(e) > (f) < (g) > (h) =
(i) < (j) <

K. (a) $\dfrac{1}{9}$ (b) $\dfrac{1}{7}$ (c) $\dfrac{1}{13}$

(d) $\dfrac{1}{11}$ (e) $\dfrac{1}{5}$ (f) $\dfrac{1}{5}$

(g) $\dfrac{3}{7}$ (h) $\dfrac{2}{9}$ (i) $\dfrac{4}{7}$

(j) $\dfrac{1}{8}$

L. (a) $\dfrac{2}{3}$ (b) $\dfrac{4}{7}$ (c) $\dfrac{11}{6}$

(d) 1 (e) $\dfrac{1}{3}$ (f) $\dfrac{4}{5}$

M. (a) $\dfrac{3}{8}$ (b) $\dfrac{2}{5}$

Test Yourself

A. 1. HCF = 15, LCM = 75
2. HCF = 8, LCM = 136
3. HCF = 10, LCM = 40
4. HCF = 4, LCM = 60
5. HCF = 7, LCM = 42

B. 1. 75 = 3×5×5
2. 88 = 2×2×2×11

C. 1. 6, 12, 18   2. 14, 28, 42

D. 1. 2   2. 1, 2, 5, 10

E. 1. $\dfrac{1}{5}$ 2. $1\dfrac{2}{9}$

3. $6\dfrac{1}{4}$ 4. $\dfrac{1}{3}$

F. 1. $\dfrac{1}{2}$ cake   2. $9\dfrac{7}{12}$ kg

3. $\dfrac{1}{4}$ 4. 2 chocolates

Geometry

A. 1. Lines = $\overleftrightarrow{PS}, \overleftrightarrow{XZ}$;
Line segments = $\overline{QR}, \overline{QY}, \overline{RY}$;
Rays = $\overrightarrow{YZ}, \overrightarrow{YX}, \overrightarrow{QP}, \overrightarrow{QS}, \overrightarrow{RP}, \overrightarrow{RS}$

2. Lines = $\overleftrightarrow{PG}$
Line segments = $\overline{AB}, \overline{BC}, \overline{CD}, \overline{AD}, \overline{QF},$
$\overline{AQ}, \overline{QB}, \overline{DF}, \overline{FC}$
Rays = $\overrightarrow{QP}, \overrightarrow{QG}, \overrightarrow{FP}, \overrightarrow{FG}$

B. 1. one   2. two
3. line   4. parallel
5. angle   6. polygon
7. quadrilaterals   8. radius
9. radius   10. circumference

C. Centre = O
Raidius = OP, OA, OB
Diameter = QB, AP
Chord = RB, TS, AP, QB

D. 1. ∠MPN, $\overrightarrow{PM}$ and $\overrightarrow{PN}$, P
2. ΔPQR, $\overrightarrow{QP}$ and $\overrightarrow{QR}$, PR
3. ∠XYZ, Y, $\overrightarrow{YX}$ and $\overrightarrow{YZ}$, V and S, T and B

www.ingramcontent.com/pod-product-compliance
Lightning Source LLC
Chambersburg PA
CBHW040056160426
43192CB00002B/85